Dialling a Starless Past

Mike McNamara

ARENIG PRESS

First published in 2019
by Arenig Ltd (Arenig Press)
Dolfawr, Cwmrheidol, Aberystwyth SY23 3NB

Printed in UK by
4Edge Ltd, 22 Eldon Way, Hockley SS5 4AD

A CIP record for this book
is available from the British Library

ISBN : 978-1-9998491-6-0

Cover: From a painting by the author

IM Fell English font digitally reproduced by Igino Marini.
www.iginomarini.com

ACKNOWLEDGEMENTS

For Theresa who, as woman and muse, deserved a finer man
and a greater poet.

Special thanks to Big Al The Encourager.

PREVIOUSLY

Selected Poems 'Overhearing The Incoherent' (*Grevatt and Grevatt*, 1997).

As well as being a published songwriter, Mike's poetry has been published in Acumen, Aji, Dream Catcher, Envoi, Eunoia Review, International Times, Ink Sweat & Tears, The Lyric, New Welsh Review, Orbis, Reach, Subterranean Blue, Tears in the Fence, etc.

Mike also had a selection of poems published in The Pterodactyl's Wing (*Parthian*, 2003). His ebook This Transmission was published in Sept. 2019 by *The Argotist Online*.

Dialling a Starless Past

Never to Return

Recalling Halstead Street
1963
the outside toilet
whitewashed walls
legs dangling in the darkness, wide eyed
scanning walls for scurrying eight legged predators
the sight of which would send me sprawling, bare arsed
into the safe moonlit back yard. Eight years old.
Never to return.

Often sat there
eyes closed, imagining
the past months
all a fevered dream
where I would awaken once again in Antrim
surrounded by familiar faces, friends and family
Ferris Park and the fields we'd played in.
Forever lost in strange accented South Wales.
Never to return.

In the kitchen
breakfast left by younger ones
impatient or slight
of appetite
a stabbed sausage, the crisp fried bread still warm.
The lino floor, the loyal sold as seen gas cooker
a coal fire spittling beneath the stone-look wallpaper.
Our would be haven off lorry laden Corporation Road.
Never to return.

The pungent tang of
my leather satchel, marked
with comforting names
of Irish uncles; far away kin.
We puffed the early morning air from frozen
untainted lungs, make believe smokers
forming the legacy of life to come;
playing grown ups until that final breath.
Never to return.

Dialling a Starless Past

Were those November nights starlit? I only sought
the darkness as I slouched by, bred from a preternatural elan
and a frying pan that would have felled a finer man
(thus refinement was declined in a blind endeavour to survive).

Looking for stars played no part in the technique
of a boy who rarely looked above the street signs.
High Street stores and bars drew me to where
council house Celtic belters rustled
efficiently in crisp overalls; catching
their dark lashed eyes my sole aim. Streetwise girls
built for Hollywood but trapped by place and time
at tills in Woolworths, Boots, Smiths.

If stars shone out I chose to let them glow
jiving at The Living Eye, mooching around the low life
dockside caffs, limping from clinics after penicillin shots
the sex roulette compulsion, pain for pleasure.

Scribbling florid lines in pre-expulsion school books
Flags Of The World cards, US Civil War banknotes.
Always a peg or a pen to be found in the bread bin
the button box a treasure trove of plastic soldiers
foreign coins, old chalk marbles. Plain, common folk
in exile from the wild North Antrim coast.

Stood up, starless on the market steps
seven No. 6 tipped in the pocket of my Sta-Prest
while the Michaelstone beauty with the crow black bob
rode shop soiled pillion on that Soul City Vespa
headed out for Detroit, Motown, west of Barnardtown.

Now I dial the past but the connecting line is dead.
The codes have changed, my coins no longer legal tender.
The In Place is derelict, the market steps a no-mans land.
Tonight, I would share my now starlit secrets with you
that shine beyond the bottled backstreets I once walked
but prison, grave and forty years divide us.

Schooldays

A maelstrom flush from glazed Shanks bowls
disturbs the bowels of the school
where, once upon a time, the morning light
from semi-rural skies would find the same
self styled prophets of No. 6 tipped
unholy, dog end reeking neophytes

behind stained glass flecked panes. Devoid
of government health warnings, blue striped
packs were pulled from blazer pockets. Pipe thin protesters
(the wild, the wounded and the worst)
complicit, defiant of a compliant elite
etching invented monikers on sour stained walls.

What songs were sung, what white hot oaths
were sworn by L plate rebels sporting
bum fluff smirks and threadbare ties?
Hurling phlegm back at threats spat through
split locked doors, where S bend lookouts watched
for ponces or prefects through murky Mandrax eyes.

Steam from kidney filtered streams
curled in the cold to waft and evaporate above
railway lines and truant fields. A ringing bell
induced a cacophony of steel tipped shoes
and murmured farewells. Cool mixed race dudes
nodding knowingly to one another.

Schooldays. Brittle vows, rivalries
fresh selves found, fragmented, lost. Repackaged
as smoothies in three button suits and Ben Sherman shirts.
Dodging in black socked and brown brogued feet
through the short but lethal minefield of youth. Boys caught
briefly in the dying clutch of common roots.

Adrift in the Asylum

Picture a sky in shades of faded denim, blue
forever 1972, a voice singing 'Vincent' on the radio
softly, and I, incarcerated in brought-from-home pyjamas
blow seventeen candles to darkness
the heir to seventeen summers and Sun Valley roll-ups
in the asylum. Painting apocalyptic horizons and
destinations for the therapist's inaccurate chart
washed up by the rhododendrons, fag-paper thin flotsam
in Levis with naked sunburnt feet and sandals
a potential rum red Nelson anaesthetized
brutalized, a vacant lot, cast adrift for decades
from the calm and on-course, the neither hot nor cold.
Lost in acid flashbacks where The Star of the Sea sits
her face obscured behind a veil of sleek black hair
beside my bed and whispers disconcertingly clear
above Jock the alcoholic's Greek alphabet recitals
her terrible lifetime indictment:
'This ship of fools sails to no harbour'.

And I, unread, untutored, a fermenting brew
of pop culture, wholly Roman lies, True Crime, Marvel comics
detention, pitch and toss, one night stands, acne
Parade, Cockade, amphetamines, barbiturates and
Spotlight bitter. The dichotomy of good and bad
accepted or rejected, perceived in chosen haunts or length of hair
straight or stoned; no Fisher King but a sullen sprat
dredged from the nets that trawled the gutter
police cells and O.D. wards
too many, too much, too soon to take true bearings
on The Trout, Old Green, The Globe; universal
docking grounds for wrecked abusers, prison fodder
scurvied bum boys with Borstal spots and tattooed swallow hands
or the bastards of idealism who see no ships, broken, bent and
crooked in the long, shanghaiing, limp arms of the law.

The foul breathed familiar of addiction laughs at myths
in mustard coloured corridors, spits on ' Sunflowers'
curses 'The Empty Chair'. Manics, depressives
alcoholics, neurotics, junkies, psychotics. . .
high flying, flying high schizophrenics plotting their course
at the non compos mentis canteen.
Witless pressed gangs, sectioned walking shadows
victims of the chemical cosh we sink like small fry
down towards the darkest weir where crazed drowning sailors
moan in hand-me-down second hand sartorial sadness
purged of mental mutineers and stripped of star or steerage
sad captains, ancient and insane mariners
who eye the east for a slumbering sun
toothless, dribbling husks with bulging, lunar, nightwatch eyes.
Laughing at silent asides the keyless pursers of cryptic monologues
word-salad profundities and meaningless, mindless mirth
sail their sound and fury ships
to unmarked destinations through howling inner storms.

God of the Locked Ward

I return, an ex-patient of these wards
en route to the canteen
with tarmac hands and working boots.
I see you by chance and our eyes meet.
I catch a glimmer of recognition
though our arcane past was dark
and I have long been discarded with the bric a brac
and attic crap you've stored in schizophrenic archives
a harbour for whipped voices of torturing saints.
Mercifully each tormentor is now laid low
with every Clozaril exorcism.

Your black ringed eyes do not deserve to bleed anew
with the opening of early wounds. I would not wish
to drag you back to futile hopes of false redemption.
We shall not speak again nor recall our
desperate revelry, singing, drunk outside the wine lodge.
Do you regret each morning, having to awaken
to this madness over and over again?

I only come with some rough road gang;
a truck driver. I have not come to play
the jaundiced, acid Christ I once aspired to be.
Not as a voice from the bottled past nor
some reincarnation of a raving cleft eared artist.
No, I come only as a child again, as Everyman
in joy and sorrow, soft as summer rain, the passion
drained from my loins, my lions teeth worn smooth
and my rivered mane shorn close.

Blind, you led me once down wild, convulsive corridors
drunk and unholy to where he watched the world
sinused, bingoed, fag fingered;
your garrulous god of the locked ward.
Benzedrined, my brain danced, a sparkling chemical cocktail.
I watched a shower of pin prick stars swirl above the lights of
tiny cities in his brylcreemed, dandruffed hair.

Aye, once we walked together on one way streets
darkening stained glass windows
knocking bolted doors in vain.
Cursed, we searched for him for even then
his simple chair was cold. God was gone
beyond the empty stairs where odd men sit
crossed by the vibrant night and blessed
with rhyming, wordless lines.

Once on Dolphin Street

Without high heels
or a saucerful of common sense
we paused, clueless in the kitchen
peering in haphazard awe
at the kinks and colours
in one another's soul.

Welcoming in the wild men
from Chepstow and Swansea or Pembroke
the dealers and their wives
playing dominoes with
laughing West Indians at
The Welcome Home.

High on powdered amphetamine poetry
chilling on flattened Ketamine chords
sharing half crazed corner shop
Kronenberg dawns and
nursing a new psychosis
that grew unchecked among us.

One strange afternoon you gave me a book and said:
' I have read this and filled it with love. Just
open the pages; there's no need to read-
the love you need is all in there for you'.
Once on Dolphin Street, for a six months long
lost weekend, that love was there - and then was gone.

An Unlikely Tune

Drinking Skol in The Dragoon, Colchester
at nineteen. An unlikely soldier with
a headful of Swedenborg, and William Blake.
The Beatles. An unlikely husband. An

unlikely father to those who only wanted
me to be the one they kissed goodbye and
waved hello to. Was there ever such a
loneliness shared by three? A few years down

the line the abandoner of vehicles
and family living on Dover beach
a 1980's Matthew Arnold bereft
of fortune or faith. A static, isolated
soul. Are there things, narcissism, aspergers

alcoholism that can afford some
rationale? Nothing left of the me that
once was and little left of you to return to.
My days play out like a song whose melody

I can never recall pinned upon a
track; I can only improvise some notes
I hope will fit the key. Each day the same:
I awake to remember I've forgotten

the words and how it goes. And I can cite
disorders or labels self diagnosed
but the emptiness is still the same. The
missing pieces remain missing. Can
someone ever tell us the title, the tune?

Skinhead Girls

Skinhead girls
who'd come to town
from maisonettes on stuccoed estates
or the crumbling dockside terraces
hard faced with fashion's feather cuts.
The Mo's, the Junes, the Irises and the rest
who scuffed up and down the old bus station at night
when the youth clubs had closed
stiff necked with folded arms
chewing gum with exaggerated distaste
involved in some angry teenage intrigue;
sorting this one out with a slap, or that one with a glare
defining pecking orders or impressing
some crowing crombied cock.

Skinhead girls
mothers' angry little helpers
(who all their lives they'd watch and mimic)
those gloveless mums
who led them to school with frozen hands
popped next door with blackened eyes
or nipped to the Offy for fags
in headscarves and lopsided slippers.
Skinhead girls, their fleeting moment of pride played out
in loafered feet and Pretty Polly tights
short skirted mohair suits
hitching rides to romance from scooter knights.
To end the same;
marrying some straight backed lad
who'd eagerly drank himself to an early grave
waistless and wasted, a dead ringer
for his old man.

Skinhead girls
scuff through broken gates to meet on the corner
 those who've survived
from the Mo's, the Junes, the Irises and the rest.
All through with fashion's feather cuts
just left with watching grandkids and hopeless hearts.
Ride again, the same green and whites to find
their town changed forever.
Not a trace remains of the names they'd scrawled
on seats and window frames

or the fickle loves they had proclaimed
etched in passion with nailfile or penknife.
All rusted now on the bus stops and derelict shelters
where no boys wait.

Soul Music

Come ride with me in the band van
on the Great North Road to Billingham.
Nov. 2nd 2018. We've just learnt
Johnny Johnson And The Bandwagon's
Breaking Down The Walls Of Heartache.

Faces in the clouds.
Yeah, ok, we create our own reality
but reality's a collective creativity-
like a band interpretation of an old song.

Powerless, unwell and bereft of hope; forced to
reconcile to a power greater than ourselves
some Jazzy Jah-like, John Coltranic deity
a forever stranger with an aural vision far beyond our own
febrile machinations. Let it go. Let it be.

Ask a hundred faces in the crowd 'Who am I?'-
a hundred voices will call out a different answer.
Where there's no right or rhythm or wrong
eternity's a split second long
there's a no- no time signature
the seer is one with the seen
and the singer becomes the song.
You know that tune?

Cold water on a winter morning, like
a verse first heard with someone who once loved you
evokes primordial, half forgotten memories.
Do those born deaf miss a tune
like the blind miss a torch
or the unburied dead mind a wasp?
I think I'll drop a downer for the long trip home.

Empty

That flat on the end of Woodland Road
where those boys once quoted Manson, Marx
or Malcolm X and drank Double Diamond
smoking thin packets of crumpled cigarettes
after the black and white tv
went blank at midnight, is empty now.

On Newport Bridge 1988

Years later now, an older man it seems
in contrast to the boy with visions lit by hopeful schemes
sated now, misled by blind addiction
but spared at least self pity for this self imposed affliction.

I dreamt in colour then but cannot now recall who dreamed
inspired by the radio and hymn like songs that seemed
to echo long ago those gospel tunes by Motown blades
with lyrics painting endless love behind those hipster shades.

Western patriarchal gods I prayed to in my youth
or Eastern koans I meditated on in my careless search for truth
tabs of acid, grams of speed or flagons of
alcohol and vomit while the needle syphoned love.

I stumbled willingly across the bridge each night,
Over the river Usk, blessing the patterns from the docked boats' light
Every winding backstreet seemed like the blueprint for some plan
That led me onward to a knowledge of the ways of man.

I walked across that bridge once more tonight
A squanderer of words and empty years and love's lost light
Just a wanderer in a 60's suit from some Dock Street Oxfam shop
Wishing with every wasted breath this cold night crossing would stop.

.

Missed

'If I rise now, there's little of consequence to do with my day
if I speak now, there's nothing of importance to say;
you and I are a million lost moments away
one from another.'

You laughed at the way I danced
you said it was like
Aiken Drum from our little girl's favourite video
or the old black man who'd get up
in that Cardiff pub, pointing at the floor
while his feet shuffled lazily.

I never told you, of course, but I loved
the sound of your laughter.
Church bell clear
untinged with malice or smugness.
There was much I didn't know
and was late in the learning;
how laughter and innocence can be neglected or nurtured
how thoughtless words or actions
can empty the fullest heart
and fill the bluest eyes with tears.

'If I could have read to you
if I could have given some me to you
if I could have wept like you
if I could have lived to
only be with you...
what then might we have discovered?'

The old man, the Cardiff pub, both long gone;
his spoons won't rattle and his feet won't shuffle there again.
Our young woman no longer sits securely between us
entranced on that old settee.
Our shared days of dance and laughter
have played out
like her childish video
distorted and warped by the passing time.

X's Are Not Real Kisses

The day when we danced has ended.
Day long days of days
long gone.
1972? 1991? 2012?
Hearing, seeing little but
writing words to you.
About you.

Thoughts in lieu of feelings;
x's are not real kisses.
Lines that lightly weigh
a shared but unshared world
stopped mid sentence
at some vague point in time.

Mercy

Endless hours of corruption
and lifetimes of worthless prayers.
A liver swollen
by terminal stupidity.
An unmasked insight that blinds.
Mercy.
Just one more hour;
just one more sentence
to be de-formed.

The Hard Man's Grave Revisited

Tomorrow I'll be as old as you were;
the unsacred mysteries you praised
as the hard, backstreet High Priest
they too are mine.
I could just make your stone, I'm still hanging.
Darkest Pill, ten years and Christchurch Hill
have maimed me.

Yeah, the dog's still with me, though my son has gone...
he has no time for talking to
the bones of men he never knew
besides
one dead drunk called
is clearly deaf enough.

Carl was killed last May
full of apple up on the Alway block.
Kenny Jay drowned pimping on the docks
his chick, the little Maltese bird split
for Neath, tattooed legs and all.
I've closed my eyes, coasting as I've slipped on down.

Since you went I've had a stint
in the city university but didn't stay.
They liked those lines about you; sharp
tutors talked of sympathy, underdogs, destiny.
They'd have felt the same, of course
if they'd crossed you, drunk and bloodied
on some misspent giro night.

A god's found Gail.
I hear her pray for you and me
the living, dying, dead. The undead.
Though spring's come round again
and ripe globes swell on young green trees
our home still reeks of old neglect.
I'm ageing in the flesh alone
as old as when the Christ went up on
one fruitless, springtime tree.

I'm sitting in the old men's bars
and young boys play our past unruly roles
in streets and alleys, clubs and pubs.
I've seen us, through windows dark with years
time and time again.
There's no retrieving mislaid hours
from sudden slipped- by days
we passed but passing
truly could have lived.

I Lean on the Door Jamb

I lean on the door jamb.
There are tiny uncultivated flowers sprouting in the back yard.
A splash of speckled colour
waiting to erupt.
Ivy clothes the fences
softening and hiding the naked edges.
And there, still bright and buoyant
a long abandoned Space Hopper
left behind by a little girl
who has gone to the moon.

In That Small House

In that small house outside Chepstow
where youthful days were pregnant
in bright streets of long ago
you said between the moments
you'd forego
the thrill and thrall of kisses
if promises and wishes
were a broken heart's placebo.

James Dewar, Loss, Addiction and E.C.T.

Now do you remember those merrydown dusks
of one lost November, ship lights on the Usk
lit snow flakes that fell like notes of a melody
in winter's white spell with port kisses of ecstasy?

(Our Caledonian bard sang us soul songs that eased
long days that wore hard and our hearts were appeased).

I see you again there on steps soft with leaves
in that coat that you'd wear with just courage beneath
braving sad tomorrows and smiling to cover
the fear of those dark clouds in one snapped forever.

If I find another in some old market town
below broken gutters where rain gurgles down
will we too pray in vain while feeding addictions
fleeing teenage pain from convulsed institutions?

They Buried Her Today The Girl Who Loved The Beatles And The Stones

The mansion was never hers
she merely seen it from afar
she said that was enough;
that ownership of things
from streets to flowers, made no sense.

She'd tease me 'Never be too busy for stillness--
you might slip between the moments of your life.'

And what a parentage!
One who renounced the world and
the other who denounced it
(and every bugger in it!).
Neither would harden
the softness of her face
the childlike wonder in her heart.

She'd ask, 'Have you seen the moon tonight?' and
'When was the last time you made someone really laugh?'

How she had wanted to believe. Belong.
From pop sock protests and concerts
to monochrome clips of Carnaby Street
on bended knees to reds or booze
idolising icons well versed in vanity or vacuity.

Anything to fill the emptiness;
to soothe the certainty of death.

From the emotional helter skelter of romantic tragedy
Eleanor Rigby, Ruby Tuesday, the zeitgeist
spiraled down to lonely TV soaps and social media.
Those high peaks became obscured in cloudy doubt
as one generation's passion morphed into a numbed

The last time we spoke she'd said an old song
She'd recognised the tune but couldn't quit

On The Brow Of The George Street Bridge

Early morning butchers
from the market with
coffee to go. Striped
aprons and stalls.

People who have things.

She always had that little princess smile
but no king to cherish her.

Heroin was the only thing
to love her.

On the brow of The George Street Bridge.
Silence.

grief.

kept playing in her head.
make out the words.

Theatre

A man's voice heard on a hill in the dark
unseen. 'I'll come back to...' carries, muffled
a woman answers, indistinct. Dogs bark
light scatters beams behind a wind ruffled

tree. A stooped man in overalls closes
a car door and walks his gravel pathway.
A Spar. A bright takeaway imposes
colours on grey slabs. A figure in sway

between the two. The park deserted. Cold.
Take a seat. No one's in until later.
Another tale's just about to unfold.
It's Friday night, here at the theatre.

The Waster Land (A Babble Of Voices)

All those seraphim prayers
to a Ridgeway god
who only listens to rich white kids.
Why should they know the angels
when the only wings we hear
are on the hungry husks of kitchen flies?

(The forests were afro hair
the sky a shiny blue of white Caucasian eye.
Those eyes were always a window to your soul
my words an empty epitaph to love.)

Bill the Traveller on rehab from the cooler
(drunk on cider at the unlamented Merry Miller)
' Let's go down The Royal Oak
have a real drink, have a smoke...
O, you can't beat the travelling boys!'

In the dark the figures glow
like scenes from Caravaggio's insight
the poetry, the poverty, one second in eternity
and the world seems full of emptiness tonight.

We had a drink before he went
that's enough for a man like me
he bought a few, I called in two
then he went home for his tea.
I later heard his time was spent
and he died that very night
but we had a drink before he went
so things turned out alright.

(Once the stairs were white
and our hair was brown
now the passing years
have turned it round. Oh, lover

now that our beauty has faded
and the dreams that we clung to are gone
I regret in an instant this evening
a lifetime of moments long gone.)

And the schizoid man said
' Cold eyes don't cry for life's losses
cold arms don't wait for returns
cold souls don't yearn for time wasted
cold hearts freeze a love when it burns.'

In the dark the figures glow
like scenes from Caravaggio's insight
the poetry, the poverty
one second in eternity
and the world seems full of yesterday tonight.

'Surely there was a time'
(said the poet from some bedsit in York Place)
'When I walked the dockside streets
free from the goals and desires
that chain me now
when the sun rose as a joy in my soul
and I laughed with the trees
and the carolling leaves?'

'But don't forget'
(said the labourer from his flat in Alway)
' That the beautiful flowers
the song of the springtime bird...
none survives without
the silent, plain brown earth that feeds them.'

In the dark the figures glow
like scenes from Caravaggio's insight,
the poetry, the poverty
one second in eternity
and the world seems full of mystery tonight.

Military Prisoner Colchester. March–Nov. 1976

Stripped of freedom once I lay
A shorn haired Huguenot
Bedded on gleaming prison floors.
Film of life outside inside
My head, tales scrawled in captive skies
Of frosty nights we'd shared
When our frozen breaths held words
That floated upwards, touched hot stars
And thawed, releasing songs in voices from our past.

Unforgotten faces.
Acid brains.
Drugless dreamers babbling
Of Glastonbury, liberty and
Planned debauchery.
Once more, in my mind returning
To tin sheds that held us
Holding up, holding on
Held hard against our will.

From Genesis to the mystic John
I chose to read
A closed book.
Blind to US fast-food culture
Deaf to fashion's voice
To Punk or passing phase.
We marched away our youth
In burning boots and barrack rooms
Trapped within these poison prison gates.

Through smoky sunsets
Shoe shine sun-ups
We looked upon a world streaked, forbidding;
Reality coated in a thin veneer of polish.
Jangling jailer's keys, hats brushed
Courtyard smeared in old mouths' spit
And glazed with a hardened shell
Of decades' sweat.
Bullshit, suffering, hate.

Insane for freedom
We made Gods from shadows
And worshipped
Writing prayers in water
Like notes from children
Burnt at Christmas
To powers
Vast
Unknown.

Metafuckingphysical

A paupered Plato stops me on the corner of Prospect Street
(itself now a dead end) and says 'Give me a reason to be.
That is my bicycle. Who am I?
I would go out if I was not depressed
if I was not depressed
I'd go out.
I can't go out.
I take the emptiness with me.'

Later, at the reading, a man with a funny hat
and a face like the stoic from that Isley Brothers song
stands up. 'Eschew the mechanistic, the scientific
the self assuredness of the cultural sophisticate
the certainties of the political adept.
Has poetry been hijacked by academic sheaf shufflers?
Is it only the well adjusted who have a tale to tell?
An articulate description of tameness
wanes into meaningless sameness.
Where is the irrational, (fuck the international)
the mysterious, the occult
the esoteric and the mystical
the metafuckingphysical?
The magic?'

Father

I saw him just once more
on that winter's night before
he left with the secret dead on Inver Hill
for one last October's long eclipse
wherein shadows all stand still.
Above dark Ireland's coast traced sea
it seemed he almost noticed me
and, for a moment, looked to say...
nothing. Raised a finger to his lips
turned, and softly ebbed away.

This Wayward Way

(No more to fall asleep a drunken god
  to awake a sober slave.)

Now, in that good tomorrow
to walk with the wisdom of midwives
bringing forth babes from Bull and Bush
milky cold to our touch.
Mother's ruin, children left not wrong
sons of fire and wrath and rock
rolling with sick thunder
Whole Lotta' Shakin' Goin' On.

Ah, without this awakening
I would lie sleepless
an uneasy bedfellow;
spilt oil on troubled waters
gutter drunk and jaundiced
from a longing for an invented long ago.

Walk me home now
old Gods of the Broken Bottle
Kings, Jesters and Priests of The Sharing Rooms;
walk me home through the by-ways
of this sober world anticipating the guttural lies
and dark denials of spirited slaves.

In a million stars above Llandrindod tonight
in the open spaces, in the misty twilight
where once I would look up at the skies
and see nothing
but the reflection of my eyes
trapped in a vacuum.

I turn, humbled. Homeward bound.

In the headlights' beam I see a road beyond
the bitter, brown topped years
where I dreamt I crawled alone
in my self deluged, deluded vale of tears
until I awoke and knew:
I was meant to be
led home this wayward way.

ARENIG PRESS
Dolfawr
Cwmrheidol
Aberystwyth
Ceredigion
SY23 3NB

www.arenig.co.uk